HISTORY IN ART

MIDDLE AGES

Raintree

FIONA MACDONALD

www.raintreepublishers.co.uk
Visit our website to find out more information about **Raintree** books.

To order:
 Phone 44 (0) 1865 888113
 Send a fax to 44 (0) 1865 314091
Visit the Raintree Bookshop at **www.raintreepublishers.co.uk** to browse our catalogue and order online.

 Produced for Raintree by
White-Thomson Publishing Ltd
Bridgewater Business Centre, 210 High Street,
Lewes, East Sussex, BN7 2NH.

First published in Great Britain by Raintree, Halley Court,
Jordan Hill, Oxford OX2 8EJ, part of Harcourt Education.
Raintree is a registered trademark of Harcourt Education Ltd.

Editorial: Cath Senker and Diyan Leake
Consultant: Dr Susan Edgington
Design: Richard Parker
Page make-up: Mind's Eye Design Ltd, Lewes
Picture Research: Elaine Fuoco-Lang
Map artwork: Encompass Graphics
Production: Amanda Meaden
Originated by Dot Gradations
Printed and bound in Hong Kong, China
by South China Printing Company

ISBN 1 844 43370 6
09 08 07 06 05
10 9 8 7 6 5 4 3 2 1

British Library Cataloguing in Publication Data
Macdonald, Fiona
History in Art: The Middle Ages
709'.02
A full catalogue record for this book is available from the
British Library.

Acknowledgements
The publishers would like to thank the following for permission to
reproduce photographs (t = top, b = bottom): Art Archive *title page*,
contents page (Museo delle Armature Brescia/Dagli Orti), pp. **5** (t)
(Torre Aquila Trento/Dagli Orti), **5** (b) (Dagli Orti), **6, 8, 9** (both),
10, 11 (t), **11** (b) (British Library), **12, 13** (t), **13** (b) (Museo delle
Armature Brescia/Dagli Orti), **14, 15** (Dagli Orti), **16, 17** (t)
(Biblioteca Nazionale Turin/Dagli Orti), **17** (b) (Canterbury Cathedral/
Jarrold Publishing), **18** (Dagli Orti), **19** (t), **19** (b) (St Stephen's
Cathedral Vienna/Dagli Orti), **20** (Museo Diocesano Orta/Dagli
Orti), **21** (t), **21** (b) (British Library), **22, 23** (Dagli Orti), **24**
(Bibliothèque Municipale Laon/Dagli Orti), **25** (t), **25** (b) (Bibliothèque
Municipale Dijon/Dagli Orti), **26** (Victoria and Albert Museum/
Graham Brandon), **27** (t), **27** (b) (British Library), **28** (Museo Civico
Bologna/Dagli Orti), **29** (British Library), **30** (Victoria and Albert
Museum/Graham Brandon), **31** (b) (Biblioteca Estense Modena/Dagli
Orti), **32** (Bibliothèque Nationale Paris/Harper Collins Publishers), **33**
(t) (University Library Prague/Dagli Orti), **33** (b) (St Sebastian Chapel
Lanslevillard Savoy/Dagli Orti), **34, 35** (Bodleian Library), **36** (Bodleian
Library), **37** (t), **37** (b) (Unterlinden Museum Colmar/Album/Joseph
Martin), **38** (National Museum Damascus Syria/Dagli Orti), **39** (b), **40**
(Vatican Museum Rome/Album/Joseph Martin), **42** (Biblioteca Estense
Modena/Harper Collins Publishers), **43** (Musée Gutenberg Mayence/
Dagli Orti), **44** (British Library), **45**; Bridgeman pp. **7, 41** (b); British
Library pp. **31** (t), **41** (t); Corbis p. **39** (t) (Nik Wheeler).

Cover photograph of a 14th-century bust of Charlemagne,
reproduced with permission of the Art Archive.

Every effort has been made to contact copyright holders of any
material reproduced in this book. Any omissions will be rectified
in subsequent printings if notice is given to the publishers.

Disclaimer
All the Internet addresses (URLs) given in this book were valid at
the time of going to press. However, due to the dynamic nature of
the Internet, some addresses may have changed, or sites may have
changed or ceased to exist since publication. While the author and
publishers regret any inconvenience this may cause readers, no
responsibility for any such changes can be accepted by either the
author or the publishers.

The paper used to print this book comes from sustainable resources.

Contents

Chapter 1 Art as evidence   4
Art and its makers   6

Chapter 2   History of the Middle Ages   8
Powerful people   10
Wars and conquests   12
Castles   14
Knights and chivalry   16

Chapter 3   Church and people   18
Rituals and festivals   20
Cathedrals   22
Monasteries   24

Chapter 4   Everyday life   26
Towns, crafts and trade   28
Homes and families   30
Good times, bad times   32
Illustrated manuscripts   34

Chapter 5 The wider world   36
International scholarship   38
New ideas, new explorations   40
Maps and printing   42

Timeline   44
Glossary   46
Further resources   47
Index   48

Words included in the glossary are in **bold** the first time they appear in each chapter.

Art as evidence

Eighteenth-century scholars looked back at the period AD 500 to 1500 as a dim, miserable middle period separating two greater, more glorious ages. They called this period the 'Middle Ages'. The scholars looked back in admiration to the civilization of ancient Rome that ended around AD 500, and admired their own times, which started with the **Renaissance** in the fifteenth century.

Mixed traditions

This book looks at art and architecture during the Middle Ages – focusing on the period from AD 1250 to 1500, for which there is more evidence. Contrary to the views of those eighteenth-century scholars, Europe was home to a rich artistic and literary culture that combined ancient **pagan** traditions with new ideas based on the Christian faith. It also absorbed influences from neighbouring Muslim and **Byzantine** (Greek) cultures, and from civilizations as far away as China and India.

All these influences can be seen – though not all at the same time – in medieval works of art. Laws, politics, social attitudes, religious beliefs and economic conditions were also reflected in medieval art and architecture. However, there is sometimes a difference between what medieval artists aimed to portray in a work of art, and what historians see in it today.

▼ The medieval world around 1200, showing places mentioned in this book.

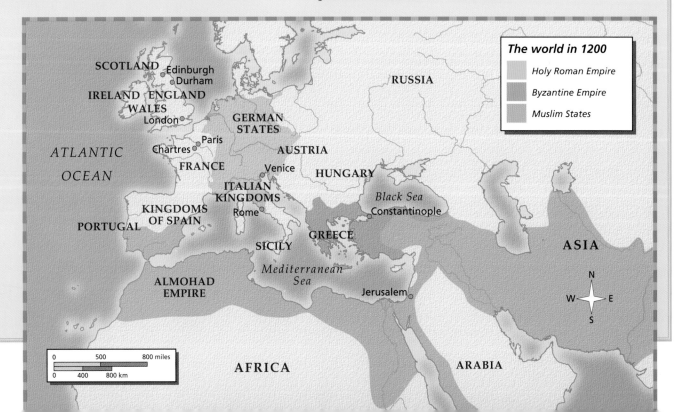

The world in 1200
- Holy Roman Empire
- Byzantine Empire
- Muslim States

SCOTLAND
Edinburgh
Durham
IRELAND ENGLAND
WALES
London
RUSSIA
GERMAN STATES
Paris
ATLANTIC OCEAN
Chartres
FRANCE
AUSTRIA
Venice
HUNGARY
ITALIAN KINGDOMS
KINGDOMS OF SPAIN
Rome
Black Sea
Constantinople
PORTUGAL
GREECE
SICILY
Mediterranean Sea
ASIA
ALMOHAD EMPIRE
Jerusalem
N
W   E
S
0   500   800 miles
0   400   800 km
AFRICA
ARABIA

▶ The month of July, pictured as a **fresco** (painting on wall plaster) by an artist in Bohemia (now part of the Czech Republic) around 1400.

Training and skills

Medieval artists were craftsmen and women who spent long years training to perfect their skills. Seven years of study and practice were not uncommon. They used a wide range of materials, including wood, stone, pottery, glass, gold and silver, precious stones, leather, cloth, wax, powdered minerals and animal horn. With these they created all kinds of wonderful objects and many splendid buildings.

▶ Medieval craftworkers created many magnificent buildings, like this cathedral in the city of Siena, Italy, completed in the thirteenth century in a mixture of artistic styles.

These *peasant* men are cutting grass to make hay

This peasant man sharpens his scythe

This is the manor house

A young **noble** man and woman, courting

The women are gathering up cut grass with rakes

A boating party out on a pond

This is a stained-glass window

Here is the bell tower

Here we can see **Gothic** (later medieval) pointed decoration

These are carved stone statues in niches (little hollows) above doors

This is the west doorway

Art and its makers

Many different kinds of art have survived from the Middle Ages. They range from tiny pieces of jewellery to tall, towering cathedrals, and from delicate **manuscript** illustrations to grim, forbidding castles and forts.

Today, we often find these medieval artefacts (created objects) very beautiful to look at. We admire their strength or their splendour, their skilled workmanship and their clever designs. They can also be looked at in another way – as historical evidence. We can use them to find out what medieval people wore, how they worshipped, where they lived, and how they fought. They can help us get a better understanding of what life was like in medieval times.

Makers and patrons

Before historians can use any work of art as evidence, they need to find out more about it. They need to know who made it, who paid for it, and why it was designed in its own particular way. We know the names of some great medieval artists, such as the Italian Simone Martini (c.1284 to c.1344), who experimented with colour and light effects in his wall paintings.

Some architects are known to us too, such as the French designer of churches Villard de Honnecourt (c.1225 to c.1250).

▼ This lifelike bronze panel, from a church doorway in Verona, Italy, shows a sculptor at work.

The wooden mallet is used to hit the chisel

This metal chisel is used to cut stone

The block of stone being carved

The sculptor sits on a wooden stool

De Honnecourt also invented elaborate machinery. Yet the names of many other skilled men and women were never written down. They laboured as part of a team in a master-craftsman's workshop, or spent their lives shut away in monasteries and nunneries.

We do, however, know much more about artists' **patrons** – the people who ordered and paid for new buildings and works of art. They belonged to two main groups: rich, powerful people, such as kings and queens or lords and ladies, and the **Christian Church**.

▼ This is one of six **tapestries** woven in France around 1500 to decorate the home of a wealthy nobleman. Five of them symbolize the senses – this one symbolizes smell. They also have a Christian religious meaning.

Examining the evidence

Medieval art is often full of lifelike details. Artists were skilled at painting all they saw around them, from villages full of muddy farmworkers to exciting tournaments (mock battles) watched by fashionable lords and ladies. They carved realistic statues of gallant heroes and suffering **saints**. In addition, they copied images from earlier artists' works, and painted unicorns, dragons and many other imaginary creatures that they had not seen with their own eyes. Sometimes, they put these into their works just for fun. More often, they used them like a secret code, to send a special message.

Here is the decorative millefiore (thousand flowers) background

*The banner displays a noble's **coat of arms***

A dog has a keen sense of smell

This garland of flowers smells sweet

The lady symbolizes the Virgin Mary, Jesus' life on earth, and his death

The enclosed garden symbolizes earthly pleasures

Here is a basket with flowers

The unicorn symbolizes Jesus Christ

Thoughts and feelings

Medieval artists sometimes used their work to express invisible things, such as thoughts, feelings, hopes and fears. They used special symbols in their work to show these. For example, white lily flowers stood for purity, and a lion symbolized courage. They also pictured forces, such as good and evil. They believed these played an important part in their world. Artists often showed these as angels and devils, sometimes fighting to control a human soul.

History of the Middle Ages

The Middle Ages started when the mighty Roman Empire collapsed. This was a long, slow, rather chaotic process that began around AD 200 when Roman emperors and army commanders started fighting among themselves to win power. It ended when invaders forced the last emperor to flee from Rome in 476.

The Roman Empire

At its greatest, around 117, the Roman Empire controlled almost all of Europe, as well as North Africa and the Middle East. Everywhere they ruled, Roman rulers introduced their own language, laws, beliefs and technology. In 313, Christians ceased to be persecuted by the Romans, and their religion spread to the lands of the empire. New churches were constructed for Christian worship, and new Christian symbols, such as the fish and the cross, began to appear in paintings, jewellery and many other works of art.

Invasions and migrations

From around 300, groups of nomadic warriors invaded Europe from the north and east. They belonged to many different peoples, including the Huns, Goths, Visigoths and Vandals. The invaders cared nothing for Roman civilization. They smashed buildings and carried away gold and silver art treasures, to melt down. Threatened by these invaders, some northern European peoples, such as the Angles and the Saxons, moved to settle in new lands, including southern Britain.

▶ Detail from an Anglo-Saxon whalebone casket carved in north-east England between 700 and 800.

A warrior with helmet, shield and spear

Metal studs hold the four sides of the casket together

This is an inscription in runes, a writing system used in northern Europe

Later, from around 800, new invaders attacked. They included Vikings from Scandinavia, who settled in north-west Europe, and Magyars from Central Asia, who made a new home in Hungary. Muslims also came from North Africa to live in southern Spain. These invaders brought their own artistic traditions with them, such as Viking metalworking skills and Muslim garden design. Muslims also brought a new kind of building to Europe – the mosque – which was their place of worship.

Holy Roman Empire

After 476, the lands of the Roman Empire were divided among many rival local kings. In western Europe, the greatest of these was Charlemagne, leader of the Frankish people who lived in France and Germany. Charlemagne was a ruthless warrior, who helped the Pope (head of the Western branch of the **Christian Church**) to defend Rome against invaders. In return, the Pope crowned him Holy Roman Emperor in 800.

Charlemagne (and later kings who claimed the same title, such as Otto the Great, who ruled Germany from 912 to 973) saw themselves as heirs to Roman traditions. Art and architecture in their kingdoms – for example, Charlemagne's new palace and chapel at Aachen, France – were strongly influenced by Roman designs. Emperors also paid for many Christian religious **manuscripts** (see pages 34–5) to be made, in a new style of handwriting based on Roman originals.

▲ A fourteenth-century bust (model of head, shoulders and chest) of the Frankish King Charlemagne, made of gold and silver.

Rome in the East

After the Roman Empire divided into eastern and western parts in 330, Roman civilization in the east was based in Constantinople (modern Istanbul). This area later became known as the **Byzantine Empire**. Byzantine artists continued many Roman traditions in architecture, such as **mosaic** decoration for floors and walls. They also added new features, such as domed roofs over square church buildings.

▶ The church of Hagia Sophia (Holy Wisdom), completed in 537, in the Byzantine capital city of Constantinople.

The four minarets were added after 1453, when Hagia Sophia was turned into a mosque

There are windows under the dome

Here is the domed roof

The arch on top of the pillars supports the dome

The rectangular hall is for Christian worship

Powerful people

When the Viking and Magyar invasions ended, soon after 1000, Europe slowly became more stable. Different peoples settled down in their own separate territories. Most were ruled by kings. Compared with rulers today, medieval kings had tremendous power – but only for as long as they could hold on to it. In some countries, all royal sons had the right to claim the throne. The strongest, or most ruthless, would win. Kings also had to fight against jealous, ambitious **nobles**, and enemies from neighbouring lands.

God's deputies

Medieval kings claimed to be God's deputies on earth. This meant they could command great respect, but they also had great responsibilities. It was each king's duty to guard his kingdom and make good laws.

The king had to protect the Christian Church, and encourage peace and prosperity. In return, he demanded loyalty from his subjects, together with service in the royal army and heavy **tolls** and taxes.

Set apart

A king's special status, and his riches and power, influenced the way he appeared in public. He was kept apart from ordinary people, and often appeared high above them on a dais (ceremonial platform) or a throne. He was dressed in elaborate robes, and wore a jewelled crown. This high status also shaped the way royalty was portrayed in medieval art. Few lifelike pictures of kings or queens were made in medieval times. Instead, artists created icons (ideal images) that made kings, queens and their families look superhuman.

▶ King Henry VI of England (lived 1421–71) receives a book from its author, poet John Lydgate.

The canopy above his head shows that the king is special

The crown is a sign of royalty

His robe is lined with valuable ermine fur, which only kings and nobles could wear

The king wears gloves, to avoid contact with ordinary people

The king is seated on a throne raised above ground level

The bodyguard stands watch, with his sword drawn

The author's tonsure (part-shaved head) shows he is a monk

The author is kneeling to show respect

10

These are the members of the ruling council, who advise the Doge

The Doge is seated on a throne and wears a rich robe, like a king

A councillor is leading the discussion

► This detail from a manuscript, painted in the Italian city of Venice, shows its ruler, called the Doge. He was elected from among the city's most important families.

This scribe (trained secretary) is also a **priest**

The scribes record the discussions

This scribe is writing on a parchment scroll, a material made from animal skin

Royal image

Whatever their actual appearance, kings were pictured as manly, strong and handsome. They were also shown holding royal symbols such as an upright sword, representing justice, or an orb and sceptre (small globe and heavy stick). Both were signs of worldly power.

Royal images, painted in rich colours and decorated with real gold, appeared at the top of important documents. After 1300, they were painted on panels of varnished wood. Idealized statues were also used to adorn royal tombs. Sometimes, the royal image was made from rare and costly materials, such as silver-gilt (a thin layer of gold on top of silver), superfine marble, or semi-precious stones, to stress the difference between kings and ordinary people.

▼ Royal justice – a convicted criminal being hanged in front of a king and his courtiers. This is from an Anglo-Saxon copy of part of the Bible, made soon after AD 1000.

The king holds a sword, a symbol of justice

The king is wearing a crown

Hangman

Courtiers discussing law with the king

Gallows

Criminal

Bishop holding crozier (long stick with curved top)

Propaganda pictures

Medieval kings used art as a way of advertising their achievements, and recording important events in their reigns. They paid for **scribes** to write royal **chronicles** (historical accounts of events), or compile collections of royal laws. These were often decorated with pictures of the king and his council, sitting in state. Kings and queens were also pictured making expensive gifts to churches and monasteries. In these images, they are sometimes shown standing close to **saints** or angels, who offer them special protection.

Wars and conquests

Medieval society was based on war. There were wars against neighbouring states, civil wars between different groups in the same country, and struggles against enemies outside Europe. For example, during the Crusades (religious wars) between 1096 and 1291, Europeans fought against Muslims in the Middle East.

Nobles

During most of the Middle Ages, armies were led by powerful nobles. In return for being given royal fiefs (large **estates** worked by **peasants**), the nobles were expected to fight bravely. They were supported by trained fighting men, known as **knights**, who promised loyalty, and were given smaller estates as a reward.

Knights and foot-soldiers

Medieval war tactics included pitched battles, sieges and terror campaigns. In battles, knights on horseback, armed with swords and lances (long spears), charged towards the enemy. They aimed to trample them to death or hack them down with swords. To fight back, opposing knights started a counter charge, while foot-soldiers tried to spear knights with their pikes (long spiked poles). After around 1300, foot-soldiers were armed with new, more dangerous weapons: longbows and crossbows. (Longbows fired wooden arrows very quickly over long distances. Crossbows fired short metal arrows called bolts with great force at close range.) Their bolts and arrows could pierce knights' armour and kill their horses.

▼ This thirteenth-century manuscript shows one of the most famous battles in French history, when Charlemagne's soldiers were defeated by Muslim troops from Spain, at Roncevaux in 778.

This prisoner has been tied to a tree

The red background symbolizes blood, but is not lifelike

The knights are portrayed in brave and heroic poses

The artist shows swords, but not the injuries they cause

The knights wear chain-mail armour and surcoats (loose robes) with heraldic badges

Siege warfare

Sieges were used to attack castles and walled towns by surrounding them so that no food, weapons or information could reach them. People trapped inside either starved to death or surrendered. Attackers also used siege engines to try to break down enemy defences. These included ballistas (giant crossbows), trebuchets (pronounced 'tre-boo-shay' – machines that hurled rocks) and battering rams (that smashed gates and walls). On their way to a battle or a siege, enemy armies often tried to cause as much terror as they could among enemy civilians. They looted (stole) food and valuable goods, burned down churches, houses and farms, and attacked defenceless people.

A partial view

War formed the subject-matter of many medieval manuscript illustrations. In them, we see brave knights, massed ranks of foot-soldiers, and different kinds of weapons – including the newly invented cannon, first used in Europe during the fourteenth century. Manuscript illustrations also show knights training for battle, army camps, war-horses, armourers' workshops, and sieges. These images provide valuable information about medieval warfare, but they do not provide a complete, or wholly accurate, picture. They mostly show battles from the victors' point of view, and do not record the noise, terror and suffering involved.

The banner shows a bear, symbol of the Swiss city of Berne

Foot-soldiers shelter behind heavy baggage-waggons

A wheeled carriage is used to transport the cannon

◄ This page from a Swiss chronicle (list of important events), dated 1483, shows soldiers with early cannon and guns.

Old-style knights on horseback are portrayed

This is a hand-held gun

Gunpowder is being loaded into the cannon

The cannon is placed at the top of the hill, to fire at the enemy below

▶ The best plate armour was made in Germany and Italy. Skilled craftsmen carefully shaped each section to fit the wearer. This suit of Italian armour dates from the fifteenth century.

Arts of war

Wealthy soldiers, such as nobles and knights, protected themselves with carefully tailored armour, and fought using expertly made swords. In the early Middle Ages, chain-mail, made of thousands of metal rings, was most common. After around 1300, it was replaced by shaped metal plates, and horse-armour was also made. Swords had pattern-welded blades, made by folding and hammering strips of metal together. Weapons and armour were often decorated with damascening (engraved patterns), burnishing (pressure-polishing) and gilding (gold decoration).

Castles

More than any other type of building, castles symbolize the Middle Ages. They date from a time when life was always uncertain. Built for war, they also served as family homes. Even though many castles only survive in a ruined state, they still impress us with their size and strength.

Wooden forts

The first castles were built around 1000. They were designed as forts from which armies could control conquered lands. Made of timber, they were often built on a motte (artificial mound) and surrounded by a bailey (fenced courtyard). Some of the earliest castles are pictured on the Bayeux **Tapestry**, a long **embroidered** panel that tells the story of the Norman Conquest of England in 1066.

Stronger in stone

After around 1100, castles began to be built of stone, with square **keeps** or donjons (central towers). Good examples can still be seen at Norwich and Castle Hedingham, both in eastern England, and the White Tower at the Tower of London. Stone castles were much stronger than wooden ones, and harder to burn down. To make them even stronger, many castles built after around 1150 had keeps that were round rather than square. These had no corners for enemies to undermine (dig underneath). Curved walls were much stronger and more difficult to damage when attacked by medieval war-machines, such as battering-rams.

▼ Clifford's Tower, in York, northern England, was built by William the Conqueror around 1070. It has a strong stone keep, on top of a motte of earth and rubble.

The stone walls are massive

There are narrow slit windows, high above the ground

The rounded walls are stronger than corners

The small doorway makes it difficult for enemies to enter quickly

The steep, sloping motte exhausts attackers, and makes it easier for defenders to see approaching enemies

Curtain walls

From around 1200, castle keeps were protected by thick stone 'curtain' walls built around them. (This is called a 'concentric' design.) Caerphilly castle in south Wales, built between 1268 and 1277, is a good example. It has two sets of walls, each with gates and watchtowers. The inner walls were built higher than the outer walls, allowing two teams of defenders to shoot arrows at attackers at the same time.

▼ Segovia Castle, in Spain, was rebuilt during the fifteenth century, in a concentric design.

The right site

The position of a castle was always important. Some were surrounded by deep **moats**, such as Bodiam Castle in Kent. Others were sited on rocky crags, for example, Edinburgh castle in Scotland. This made them even more difficult to attack. Knights charging on horseback could not harm them, and it was almost impossible for soldiers to climb over the walls. If defenders saw attackers trying to get in, they could push them off using long, forked poles.

From fortress to home

Towards the end of the Middle Ages, castles also became splendid homes for wealthy nobles and knights, and powerful status symbols. New castles, such as Würtemburg in what is now Lichtenstein, and Hochosterwitz in modern-day Austria, were built with pleasant private living quarters. They contained great halls for entertaining guests, chapels, guardrooms, kitchens, workrooms, and even gardens. Old castles like the Tower of London and Windsor Castle, both in southern England, were converted to make them more comfortable.

The pointed roofs on towers are a late medieval fashion

The keep has living accommodation

This is the inner wall

There are windows for lookouts

The battlements help those inside the castle to defend the walls

This is the outer wall

Knights and chivalry

The first knights were tough fighting men. They won rewards for their skill with weapons and their bravery in battle, and became wealthy enough to own war-horses, weapons and armour. Yet they were sometimes rough, crude and cruel. They built castles, and gave money to churches, but few had much interest in other works of art.

Extra duties

Around 1200, knighthood began to change. Many knights still served as officers in royal armies, or as military advisers to kings. However, some rich men paid a large fine to avoid battle duty. Other knights took on new, peaceful, responsibilities, such as serving as **members of parliament** or keeping the peace in their local communities. Training as a knight, which began in childhood, now included learning social skills, such as welcoming guests and waiting at table, as well as handling weapons and riding warhorses.

Chivalry

Slowly, a new culture of knighthood developed. It was known as 'chivalry' (from the French word *cheval*, meaning 'horse'), and was shaped by fashions in literature and Christian teachings. Chivalrous knights were meant to defend the Church, protect the weak and honour women.

▼ Knights jousting (fighting in single combat) at a tournament, shown in a fourteenth-century German manuscript illustration.

A knight has been injured by his opponent's lance

This is a wood and metal lance

The helmet covers the face, so without his shield the knight would be unrecognizable

The shield displays a coat of arms

The horse also wears a coat of arms (see opposite page)

These high ideals had little effect in real battles – but they did have a powerful impact on medieval art. Paintings, manuscripts and stained-glass windows showed knights vowing love and loyalty to ladies, or kneeling in prayer. Medieval artists also pictured glamorous tournaments – mock battles, fought with elaborate ceremony, for entertainment and as training for war.

A whole new art form, known as heraldry, grew up to record '**coats of arms**'. These were the picture-symbols worn by knights to show which family they belonged to, or which noble lord they supported. Coats of arms became signs of high rank, and were used to decorate objects belonging to knights' families, from shields and helmets to wall-paintings, tapestries and carved stone fireplaces in their homes.

By the late Middle Ages, knighthood had little connection with fighting skills. Kings made men knights to reward achievements in politics or administration. They created **fellowships** of knights, such as the 'Order of the Golden Fleece' (founded 1429–30 in what is now Belgium), for their friends and councillors (advisers). Members were not expected to fight. Fellowship meetings were recorded in sumptuous paintings and manuscripts; members wore magnificent robes or gold chains bearing the badge of their order.

▼ This is a brass tomb-effigy (lifelike statue on top of a tomb) of the famous English royal warrior, Edward, the Black Prince (1330–76).

▼ This illustration from a fifteenth-century French manuscript shows a gathering of the Knights of the Round Table. They were the heroes – and villains – of many romantic adventure stories written in medieval times.

Coronets show that knights come from royal families. Four of them are kings!

Hand gestures show courtesy and elegant manners while knights speak to each other

Rich robes show wealth

The round table shows that knights are all brothers, worthy of equal respect

A lasting memorial

Knights wanted to make sure that their fame and achievements were remembered after they died. So they commissioned artists to create memorial statues or brasses (detailed portraits, cut from polished metal), to be placed above their tombs. Most date from around 1200. They show knights dressed in their best armour, and display their coats of arms. Sometimes, a matching memorial to the knight's wife lies by his side.

Church and people

At the start of the Middle Ages, most European peoples worshipped ancient local gods and goddesses. They believed these deities controlled the weather and brought good harvests. To convert these **pagan** peoples, Christian leaders, based in Rome, sent **missionaries** all over Europe.

The Christian message

The **Christian Church** taught that Jesus Christ, a Jewish religious teacher executed around AD 30, was the Son of God. He had lived on earth to show people the right way to behave. Then, by suffering an agonizing death, He had 'saved' them. If Christians followed His teachings, and obeyed the rules made by Church leaders, they would win life after death in heaven. If they refused, they would be punished for ever in hell. These ideas gave the Church great power over people's thoughts.

Other faiths

By around AD 1000, most people in Europe were familiar with the Christian message. There were also Jewish communities, who lived in cities and towns, and Muslims, who had settled in southern Spain. Generally, the Jews were well integrated with the townspeople among whom they lived. In southern Spain, Christian, Jewish and Muslim artists and craftspeople often worked side by side. Yet from the First Crusade (1095–99) onwards the Jews were subjected to **persecution** by outsiders.

▼ *Mihrab* (niche showing the direction of the Muslim holy city, Makkah) in the mosque in Córdoba, Spain.

Geometric decoration is used because Islam forbids religious pictures of people and animals

*The **mosaics** are in **Byzantine** style, created by Christian workmen*

The mosaic patterns are based on leaves and trees

The horseshoe-shaped arch is typical of Spanish-Muslim architecture

The carved plaster decoration has been copied from Muslim architecture in North Africa and Iraq

When the Spanish Christian monarchs Ferdinand and Isabella completed the reconquest of Spain in 1492, the Muslims and Jews were expelled from the country.

Religious scenes

Christian teachings formed the subject-matter for countless works of art produced after around 800. Scenes from Jesus Christ's life, Bible stories and visions of heaven and hell decorated the walls and windows of cathedrals and churches. They were also carved in wood or stone, **cast** in gold and silver and **embroidered** in silk thread. Such images appeared in brilliant colours on the pages of illuminated **manuscripts** – handwritten books decorated with small pictures. Towards the end of the Middle Ages, they were also painted on wooden panels using oil-based paints.

Changing styles

During the Middle Ages, styles of Christian art changed. Early works often incorporated pre-Christian elements. For example, the *Book of Kells*, made around 800, has pages decorated with interlaced patterns based on **Celtic** designs. Late medieval art, after around 1350, often portrays Christ and the **saints** in a very natural style. They are pictured wearing the latest clothes, and set against fifteenth-century backgrounds. Medieval viewers would recognize and relate to these images.

▼ Images of Jesus Christ suffering death by crucifixion were displayed in all Christian churches, and in many other places in medieval times. This painted wooden panel was made in Italy, soon after 1200.

This is God in heaven

Jesus' hands are nailed to the cross

The halo is a sign that Jesus is holy

Here is Jesus' mother, the Virgin Mary

This is one of Jesus' disciples (followers), St John

There are nails through Jesus' feet

▶ This is a stone carving showing a baptism, from a font (container for holy water) at St Stephen's Cathedral, Vienna, Austria, made around 1481.

The **priest** is conducting the baptism

'Poor man's Bible'

Christian works of art were designed to remind onlookers of the Christian message. They often presented information in a very dramatic way, to achieve maximum emotional impact. The images were especially important as a source of knowledge for ordinary men and women, who could not read or write. For this reason, stained-glass windows or wall-paintings showing Christian scenes were often known as 'the poor man's Bible'.

Rituals and festivals

In medieval Europe, Christian church services and ceremonies marked the days of the week, the seasons of the year, and all the most important stages in an individual's lifetime, from the cradle to the grave.

The most important Christian ceremonies were called 'sacraments' (holy things). All of them were portrayed in medieval art. Many rich and beautiful objects were also made for use in the ceremonies. For example, holy water for baptism was contained in carved stone basins called fonts. Holy oil was carried in glass or silver flasks. Priests celebrating communion dressed in embroidered robes and knelt at an altar (holy table) covered with silk and topped by elaborate candlesticks.

The Seven Sacraments

1 Baptism – dipping in water – welcomed a new child into the Christian community.
2 Confirmation – blessing by a **bishop** – strengthened a young person's faith.
3 Communion – eating tiny pieces of bread believed to be the body of Christ – was the most solemn Christian sacrament. Priests celebrated this every day, but ordinary people took part only at Easter, or on rare, dangerous occasions, such as before battle, or when about to give birth.
4 Penance was a ceremony to show sorrow for past sins.
5 Marriage joined two Christians together in the eyes of God.
6 Ordination set men apart from the rest of the world as priests devoted to God's service.
7 Extreme unction – marking with holy oil – was a special blessing for people who were dying.

▶ A bishop saying Mass (celebrating the sacrament of communion), shown in a fifteenth-century French manuscript.

The bishop's hands are raised in blessing

The bishop's robe is embroidered with a gold cross

This is a crucifix, a statue of Jesus being killed on the cross

The altar is covered with fine silk cloth (red) and linen (white)

An angel brings a message from God

The monk helps the bishop

The light of the candle was a sign of truth and holiness

This is a missal (a book with the words of the communion service)

The king kneels to show reverence to God

20

'Magic' relics

Most ordinary medieval people did not understand their faith at a deep level. Instead, they were **superstitious**. For example, they believed that holy places, or **relics** (carefully preserved physical remains) had magic powers of their own. So they housed these relics in magnificent containers, made of gold, silver, crystal, enamel and precious stones, and went on pilgrimages to kiss or touch them.

◄ This reliquary (container for relics) was made in France between 1200 and 1300, from copper covered with real gold. It is decorated with pictures of Jesus, the Virgin Mary and four saints. The pictures are made from enamel – a mixture of chemicals that, when heated, melts to form a thin layer of coloured glass.

Living Christian lives

Church leaders encouraged many other kinds of Christian behaviour, such as giving to charity, caring for the sick, and saying prayers for the souls of the dead. Medieval people also went on pilgrimages (religious journeys) to holy places, often where saints were buried.

Medieval people liked to own small, personal, works of art. Household crucifixes (statues of Christ on the cross) and statues of the Virgin Mary, his mother, were delicately carved from wood. Rosaries – strings of beads used to count prayers – might be made of semi-precious stones. Ordinary people wore cheap metal brooches with religious designs. They purchased souvenir badges, showing emblems (images) of saints, when they went on pilgrimage.

▶ This fifteenth-century painting shows pilgrims travelling to Canterbury Cathedral, in south-east England. The relics of St Thomas Becket were preserved there. Medieval people believed they had miraculous powers.

Here are the city walls

This is the city of London

This is the old St Paul's church

The pilgrim rides on horseback

Pilgrims wore thick robes and hats with hoods, for protection from the weather

Women went on pilgrimages, and faced hardships alongside men

This pilgrim rides a mule

The road is rough and unsurfaced

21

Cathedrals

Cathedrals are some of the most splendid achievements of medieval times. Even today, when high-rise buildings dominate many cities, we can still see cathedral towers and spires soaring high into the sky. The tallest, such as Salisbury cathedral in England, are over 120 metres high. Medieval people called them 'pointers to heaven'.

The bishop's throne

A cathedral was the church from which a bishop (senior priest) ran his diocese (wide area of territory). Each one housed an impressive throne where the bishop sat while conducting important Church business, or making solemn pronouncements on religious matters. The name 'cathedral' comes from an ancient Greek word *cathedra*, which means 'seat'.

Bishops were responsible for the spiritual life of their diocese. They also had non-religious duties, as administrators and lawyers. The medieval Church was very wealthy; it owned land and collected tithes (compulsory 'gifts') from everyone. It also had its own laws governing personal behaviour, from swearing to heresy (wrong belief) and witchcraft.

▼ The interior of the **Romanesque** church at San Gimignano, Italy, built during the twelfth century.

These round arches are made of coloured stone

The stone pillars were copied from ancient Roman buildings

The barrel-shaped roof is made of rounded arches

Rows of pillars topped by arches hold up the roof

The pillars have decorated capitals (tops) in ancient Roman style

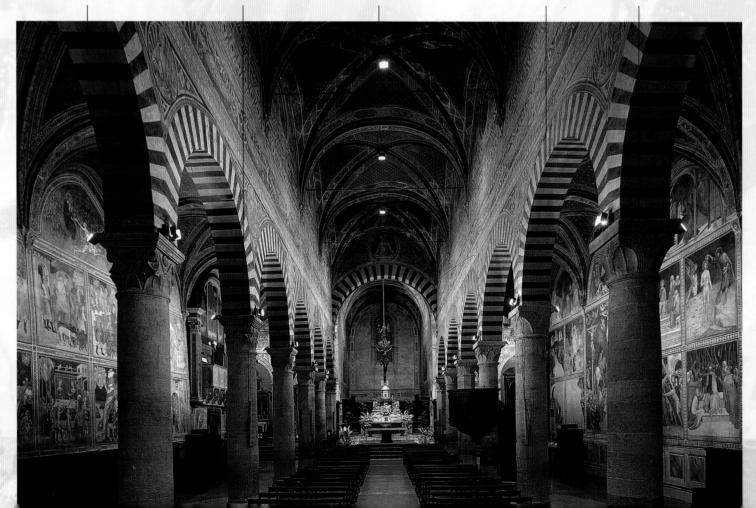

Power and glory

Cathedrals were designed to give glory to God. They also displayed the Church's power, and advertised the importance of the cities where they were built. The earliest cathedrals were paid for by kings, or from money collected by ambitious church leaders. Later in the Middle Ages, wealthy **nobles** and citizens also contributed. All these factors were reflected in the expensive materials, such as carved stone and stained glass, used to build cathedrals, and in cathedrals' bold designs.

Cathedral design

Like other medieval churches, cathedrals contained several separate parts. The nave, at the west end, was a large hall where worshippers stood. There were no seats for ordinary people. The chancel, choir and sanctuary, at the east end, were holy spaces, where monks chanted hymns and priests performed sacred ceremonies. Many cathedrals were planned in the shape of a cross, with two transepts (side-buildings) jutting out on either side of the nave.

From Romanesque...

In the early Middle Ages, cathedrals were built in Romanesque style. As its name suggests, this developed from earlier Roman designs. Romanesque cathedrals, such as Durham in England, had thick walls and massive stone pillars. These supported low, heavy, barrel-shaped roofs with round arches. For strength, walls had only small windows, creating a dark and solemn atmosphere inside. But pillars, walls and arches were decorated with lively geometric patterns, such as zigzags and V-shaped chevrons.

... to Gothic

After around 1200, cathedrals throughout Europe were built in **Gothic** style, which was very different. This was pioneered in France, at cathedrals such as Rheims, Chartres, and Nôtre-Dame in Paris. Gothic cathedrals were light and airy, with thin stone walls, pierced by enormous stained-glass windows. They were propped up by strong buttresses (stone braces) from the outside. Inside, slender, elegant columns soared up towards high roofs made of rib-vaulting – a delicate pattern of pointed stone arches covered with thin stone tiles.

▼ The west front of Nôtre-Dame Cathedral, Rheims, France, which was completed around 1310. It is one of the greatest buildings in Gothic style.

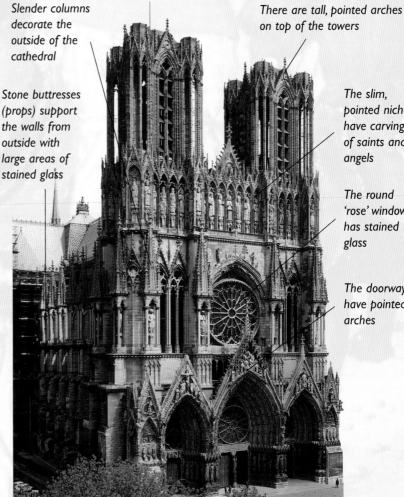

Slender columns decorate the outside of the cathedral

Stone buttresses (props) support the walls from outside with large areas of stained glass

There are tall, pointed arches on top of the towers

The slim, pointed niches have carvings of saints and angels

The round 'rose' window has stained glass

The doorways have pointed arches

Monasteries

Christian leaders taught that the world was a sinful, miserable place, but it could be improved by the power of prayer. They encouraged men and women to become monks and nuns, living shut away from the rest of the world to devote their lives to God.

Binding promises

Monks and nuns usually joined a monastery or a nunnery (religious community) when they were young, and stayed there for life. After a year spent as a novice – a trainee – a monk or nun made three solemn vows: poverty (owning no property), chastity (having no sex), and obedience (obeying the orders of their community leader). These were meant to bind them for life.

Monastic rules

There were several different orders (**fellowships**) of monks and nuns. Each was founded by a powerful leader, who laid down rules. The largest order was the **Benedictines**, founded by St Benedict (*c.*480 to *c.*547), who lived in Italy. He instructed his monks and nuns to spend one-third of their time working, one-third sleeping, and one-third praying. Later orders of monks and nuns, such as the Cistercians, founded by St Robert of Molesme, believed that hard work was a form of prayer. They built monasteries in wild, remote areas of countryside, where they kept large flocks of sheep.

▶ In the early Middle Ages, parents gave children to the Church, to train as monks or nuns. The children had no choice. This illustration from a thirteenth-century French manuscript shows a boy being given to a monastery by his father.

This is the gateway to the monastery

The monk has a tonsure (part-shaved head)

This is the boy's father

This man is a servant

Here is a monk

Schools and universities

Monks and nuns ran schools for young children, who sometimes lived in monasteries and nunneries as boarders. After around 1200, the most learned monks also left their monasteries to teach at the new universities being founded throughout Europe. Students – all male – lived in colleges that resembled small monasteries, with a chapel, a library, a dining hall, cloisters, and dormitories, or single 'cells'.

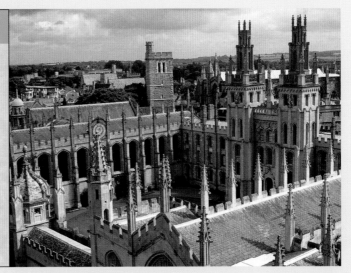

◀ New College, Oxford University, was founded in 1379. The students' rooms were arranged around a peaceful, private open space called a quadrangle. The entrance is guarded by an imposing stone gateway.

Powerful patrons

Over the centuries, monks and nuns were supported by many rich and powerful **patrons**, who helped them build splendid monasteries and nunneries. Each had a church, a chapter-house (meeting room), refectory (dining room), dormitories, a hospital, a kitchen, **cloisters** (covered walkway) and gardens for growing vegetables and medicinal herbs. Wealthy monasteries had a library and sometimes a special workroom, called a scriptorium, where manuscripts were created. The richest monasteries were built of stone, and their churches were beautifully decorated with paintings, statues, colourful clay-tiled floors and carved wooden stalls (seats).

The most famous **Benedictine** monastery was at Cluny, in France. It was built soon after 910, in Romanesque style. Later orders of monks built their monasteries in Gothic style. After around 1300, new groups of wandering missionary priests, known as friars (brothers), were founded in Italy by St Francis of Assisi and St Dominic. They built huge churches, mostly in towns, to house the crowds who came to hear them preach, with living quarters for themselves nearby. Friary churches were usually plain and simple, with wide naves (large halls) and large windows. The walls were often decorated with dramatic paintings of heaven and hell.

▼ Cistercian monks hard at work chopping wood, pictured in a twelfth-century manuscript painted at St Bernard's monastery at Clairvaux, France.

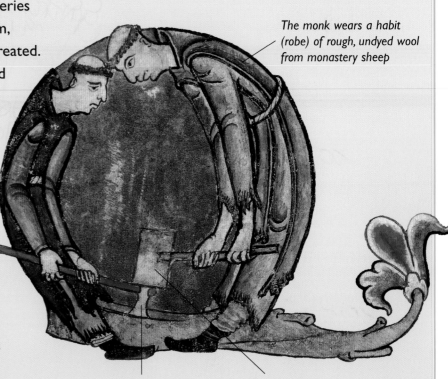

The monk wears a habit (robe) of rough, undyed wool from monastery sheep

This is a sharp metal axe   *A wooden mallet*

Everyday life

Throughout the Middle Ages, most men, women and children lived in the countryside. They worked on the land, growing crops and rearing animals. Their lives were short and hard. They produced food to feed themselves and their local lords, and if possible a surplus – a little extra to sell to people in towns.

Peasants

Farmers also produced many other essential items, such as wool and hides (to make leather clothing and footwear), wax and tallow (for candles), and timber (for ships, carts, buildings and furniture).

In spite of their vital work, **peasants** were despised by other groups in medieval society. Most peasants worked on **estates** owned by **nobles** and **knights**. In return, they were allowed to occupy small cottages of timber or rough stone, and farm little plots of land. Some peasants were legally free, but many peasants 'belonged' to their local lord. They could not change jobs, move house or even marry without his permission. Nobles and knights also collected rents and taxes from peasant families living on their lands.

▼ A peasant farmer and his wife, portrayed in a fifteenth-century French **manuscript**. He is sowing (planting) grains of wheat; she is carrying a heavy sack of wheat grains on her shoulders.

This is a sack of wheat grains

This is a peasant farmer

The border of the manuscript page is decorated with pictures of leaves and flowers

The farmer's wife's clothes look unnaturally neat and clean

Grains of wheat fall on to the ground

In real life, these clean white socks would have been dirty and muddy

The field has been ploughed

Picturing peasants

Although hardly any examples of peasant arts or crafts survive, we know that they once existed. Peasant women wove wool and linen cloth, and made garlands of flowers to wear. Peasant men plaited little figures out of straw, which they believed would protect barns and stables, and whittled wood to make spoons and bowls.

Many works by medieval artists are decorated with pictures of peasants. These pictures are usually charming, colourful and gently humorous. The peasants themselves appear well-fed and content. However, we know from other sources, such as poems, plays and legal documents, that peasants often complained, and even rebelled against their lords. Why, then, did medieval artists show them in such an unrealistic way? It is clear that the rich people who paid for these pictures knew little about peasant life.

▼ A man hoeing and a woman spinning, shown on a **fresco** on a ceiling in Norway, around 1200.

▼ 'July', from a series of fifteenth-century manuscript illustrations showing the 'Labours of the Months' in Flanders (now Belgium).

Here is part of the farmhouse

A skilled workman shears (clips wool from) a sheep

This is the stable

The next sheep is waiting to be sheared

The border of the manuscript page is decorated with paintings of wildlife and plants

The sheep's legs are tied together, to stop it running away

The workman uses metal shears

The basket is full of shorn (cut off) fleece

All year round

One favourite theme for medieval artists was 'the Labours of the Months': twelve images portraying farm work all round the year. In autumn, they show peasants ploughing fields and scattering grain. In winter they usually show a well-to-do character fattening pigs, slaughtering them, and eating them. In spring, workers weed crops, plant vegetables, care for lambs and calves, milk sheep and cows, and make butter and cheese. In summer, they make hay, harvest grain, and pick apples and pears.

The teachings of the Church said that the countryside, with its seasons, had been created by God, and that farm work was part of God's plan. So these images of the country also carried a moral message. For example, autumn scenes of picking grapes and making wine symbolized Jesus' bloody death, and how it had saved Christians from sin.

Towns, crafts and trade

By around 1200, about one in five of all European people lived and worked in a city or town. Some had been born there, but many others had migrated from the countryside. Europe's largest city was Paris, in France; it housed around 200,000 people in 1300. There were also thousands of smaller towns. Some had grown up naturally, at safe harbours or beside long-distance tracks. Others had been founded by kings and lords.

Buying and selling

Whatever their size or their origins, all European towns had one thing in common: their most important activity was trade. Medieval traders sold an astonishing range of items. Everyday goods, such as food, drink, farm tools and cooking pots, were produced locally. Many luxury goods, such as silks, spices, furs, wines and incense (sticks burned to create sweet-smelling smoke), were imported from far-distant lands.

▼ The busy cloth market at Ravenna, Italy, pictured in a manuscript made soon after 1400.

A customer tries on a coat

This is a cloth merchant's customer

Cloth is for sale on the market stall

Tailors are at their stall

A hat-maker sews a hood

This woman is buying a length of cloth

Here are sheepskins and furs for sale

▼ Blacksmiths at work in their forge, from a manuscript painted in the Netherlands around 1350.

The bellows are used to fan the flames

This is the hearth

Here is the master blacksmith

This is the blacksmith's hammer

Charcoal is used as fuel

The tongs are used for handling the hot metal

The bar of iron has been heated

This is the anvil, on which the metal is worked

Made by hand

Towns and cities were also centres of manufacturing. Skilled craftspeople made all kinds of goods, from cloth, candles and coffins to fine weapons, jewellery and furnishings. Male craft workers (and a few women) belonged to brotherhoods, called guilds. They worked together to maintain high standards, improve wages and working conditions, and care for members when they were old or ill. They also supervised a three-stage training process, from apprentice (trainee), to journeyman (qualified worker, paid by the day) and finally master-craftsman.

Town plans

Trade was so important that it shaped the layout and architecture of medieval towns. Most had a market place close to the centre where traders could set up their stalls, and some had a fairground. In wealthy towns, there might also be a covered market, sheltered by a permanent roof, or a trading hall. Merchants and craft workers could display valuable goods for sale there. Public places like these were built in grand style, using the best local materials, as a symbol of each town's wealth and pride.

Most market places also had a tall cross, or a statue of a favourite **saint**, to watch over traders and customers. The largest cities and towns were protected by strong walls with gates that were locked after dark. Space within town walls was limited, so town buildings were much taller and narrower than country ones.

Shops and houses

Most craftsmen and women worked at home, and used the front room of their house as a shop. This often had one window facing on to the street, with wooden shutters that could be let down as a counter. Many houses had workshops and storage space at the back.

Ordinary families' homes were made of timber and plaster, with thatched or tiled roofs. Wealthy merchants could afford large homes, built of stone and decorated with carved wood and painted plaster. They had showrooms for receiving favoured customers, and counting houses – rooms for writing letters and doing their accounts.

Merchants also built huge, barn-like warehouses, close to harbours or busy roads, to store their goods before sale.

Homes and families

In medieval times, there was a vast difference in living conditions between rich noble families and ordinary people, who were poor. Yet all medieval men, women and children depended on their families to survive.

Getting married

Rich noble boys and girls married young – soon after twelve years old. Their families chose their partners, for political or business reasons. Pictures of their weddings survive in many different formats – from paintings and manuscripts to decorated **ceramics**. Most were designed to record alliances between important families, rather than to celebrate love between the newly married couple.

Huge households

Rich and noble families often had six or more children – and many more servants, such as cooks, chambermaids, grooms, gardeners and bodyguards. They might also have a **priest**, children's nurses and tutors, washerwomen, secretaries and entertainers. It was a noblewoman's task to manage all these servants, entertain important visitors, and do all she could to help her husband's family gain more land or win power.

Many noblewomen also found time to become **patrons** of art or scholarship. They are often pictured in the books or manuscripts they paid for. We see them at home, in a comfortable, richly furnished chamber, being presented by the writer or artist with the finished work.

▼ Inside a comfortable home belonging to a rich French family, around 1480.

A fabric wall-hanging keeps out draughts

The walls are made of stone

These glass windows were a great luxury in those days!

The fire is in a stone fireplace

There is carved wood panelling

Fire-irons hold burning logs in place

A servant brings firewood

There is a wooden chair

The floor is tiled

Other images of wealthy lifestyles appear in portraits of favourite saints. Whatever saints' lives were actually like, artists showed them as rich people, as a sign of respect. In medieval paintings, they are wearing long robes trimmed with silk and fur, seated in rooms with carved wooden furniture, stone fireplaces, glass windows, carpets and curtains.

Simple lives

Ordinary people married much later, sometimes waiting until they were almost 30 so they could save up enough to buy simple furniture, such as wicker baskets, wooden stools or a trestle-table (a board laid on supports). They had greater freedom to choose a partner, but family approval was still important.

Generally, they had smaller families (two or three children), and lived in simple one or two-roomed houses. Beds were straw mattresses, windows were holes closed by wooden shutters, and meals were cooked in a pot hanging over a fire.

Few medieval peasant houses have survived unchanged. Good evidence of them comes from archaeological sources, and there is some evidence from medieval illustrations. By the fourteenth century, domestic scenes were popular in books on cookery, health care, farming and gardening, as well as in religious works. Yet they should be viewed with caution, as should all illustrations of peasants.

▼ A craftsman's home, pictured in a fifteenth-century manuscript showing the Holy Family. The family lives and works in one room, and the furniture is simple.

The carpenter's tools

The carpenter is smoothing wood using a plane

The young child has a pet bird

This woman is **embroidering** a piece of white linen cloth

The basket contains sewing implements

The Holy Family

Some of the clearest images of ordinary homes and families appear in religious art, depicting Jesus' early life. He is often shown as a young child playing, while His parents, Mary and Joseph, are busy at work. The Holy Family's home is pictured as a typical skilled craftsman's house – but neater, cleaner and more peaceful.

◄ The Holy Family – Mary, Joseph, and Jesus as a young child – pictured in an illustrated Bible, made in Italy around 1450. The artist, Marco dell'Avrogado, has shown a simply furnished room, typical of many peasant homes. He has added a stone fireplace and gold-topped marble columns, which peasant homes did not have!

31

Good times, bad times

There were many Christian holidays (holy days) commemorating saints' festivals, or events in Jesus' life such as Christmas and Easter. These holy days were welcome holidays for working people. They were celebrated with special services. Works of religious art, such as crosses, banners and statues, were carried through the streets, and there were games, dancing and religious plays.

▼ Hunting was the favourite sport of most noblemen – and many noblewomen. This illustration of stag-hunting comes from a book written in France around 1410.

Noble pleasures

Kings and wealthy nobles employed professional poets, minstrels (musical entertainers) and jesters (clowns). Chess was introduced from the Middle East before 1000, and became popular among nobles. Pieces and boards were often elaborately carved and painted. Other noble pastimes, such as hunting and hawking, were portrayed on wall paintings and **tapestries**. More down-to-earth entertainers, such as jugglers and acrobats who performed at markets and fairs, wore brightly coloured, eye-catching costumes, decorated with little bells.

The huntsmen blow hunting-horns

The nobleman rides a fast horse

The huntsmen are encouraging the hounds

The stag is running into the forest

The hounds chase the stag

Death and disaster

Between 1347 and 1351, medieval Europe suffered an enormous shock. Around one-third of its people were killed by an infectious disease that was caused by deadly bacteria (germs) carried by rats and fleas. Medieval people called it the 'pestilence', or plague. Many thought that the end of the world had come.

Even after the worst outbreaks of plague had ended, many people were still frightened. Anxiety was increased because no one understood how the disease spread, or how it could be prevented. Late-medieval people lived in constant fear that it might soon be their turn to catch the disease.

▼ Medieval people believed that blood-letting (cutting open veins so that the blood poured out) could cure many diseases. This illustration from a Czech medical manuscript was made around 1450.

▶ A doctor treating victims of plague, from a **fresco** in a chapel in Savoy (south-eastern France), made in the fifteenth century.

A sense of doom

To try to fend off further plague attacks, medieval men and women joined **fellowships**, groups who punished themselves, went without food, or organized prayers and processions. They gave money to churches to pay for memorials to dead friends and family members. These often portrayed people as dead bodies in shrouds (sheet-like wrappings), or even as skeletons, rather than as they had looked in the prime of life. Individuals and fellowships paid for statues and paintings of guardian saints (who, it was believed, watched over the community) to be placed in churches. There were also many '**Doom**' paintings, showing dead Christians' souls being checked at the Last Judgement, together with blissful images of heaven, and fearsome, gaping monsters representing the gateway to hell.

'Memento mori' (Reminders of death)

Many late-medieval manuscripts were decorated with illustrations of sudden death, as an awful warning to readers to live good Christian lives – because tomorrow they might die. Some of these showed a chilling *danse macabre* (grisly dance), in which grinning skeletons carried off living dancers. Other images included the 'three living and the three dead', a scene in which three travellers come face-to-face with their own corpses. More comforting images, such as statues of the Virgin Mary and gentle female saints, were also popular in churches and private homes.

The angel and devil are waiting to snatch the souls of plague victims when they die

This man, with a plague bubo (swelling) in his armpit, is waiting to see the doctor

This young boy is crying because his parents are ill

The doctor is cutting open a plague bubo on the woman's neck

The baby in the cradle will starve if its mother dies from plague

Illustrated manuscripts

M any monks, and some nuns, were well educated. They compiled **chronicles**, and made copies of religious books and manuscripts. They decorated these with religious pictures or carefully observed scenes from everyday life. Many examples of monks' work still survive today, and are an important source of evidence for medieval life.

Books and manuscripts

Monks wrote and copied texts to make manuscripts (the word means 'written by hand'). They were often decorated with pictures in the margins, or at the beginning of chapters, paragraphs and important sentences. Most manuscripts were created as long scrolls or single sheets. But some were collected together and bound between covers to make books. This was either done straight away, or some time after they were first written. After around 1200, purpose-designed, hand-written, books became more popular, because they were easier to read.

When creating books and manuscripts, monks wrote on specially prepared lengths of vellum (calf-skin) or parchment (sheepskin) that had been soaked, scraped clean of flesh and hair, stretched and smoothed. They used goose-feather quills and inks made from soot and oak-gall (the swelling on an oak-tree twig, caused by an insect, which was dried and crushed to make a dark dye). Their paints were made from crushed minerals such as brilliant blue lapis lazuli and bright red minium (lead oxide) mixed with glue. This, and not their small size, gave medieval 'miniature' paintings their name.

▼ A fifteenth-century monk creating an illuminated manuscript in the scriptorium (writing-room) of his monastery.

The books are stored on shelves

A curtain protects books from dust and from bright sunlight, which would fade them

A magnifying glass helped with very detailed work

This is a quill pen (central rib of a feather)

The sloping wooden desk is on an adjustable metal stand

This is St Veronica. Medieval legends told how she wiped Jesus' face with a cloth, and his image appeared on it

Most of the page is decorated

The border of the page is decorated

The written text is a prayer

This space is left blank for the book owner's **coat of arms**

▲ Two pages from a Book of Hours made for Flemish (Belgian) nobleman Philippe de Conrault around 1480. Each is decorated with lifelike pictures of flowers and insects.

For religious images, real gold leaf was sometimes added, to give glory to God. To guide their writing, and keep it straight on the page, they ruled lines with a stylus (bone or metal pointer). This made a slight groove in the surface of the vellum or parchment; writers could feel it, but it was not easy for readers to see.

Styles of illustration changed over the centuries, and often reflected changing fashions in architecture. Early medieval manuscripts use rounded, **Romanesque**-style decorations, and deep, rich colours. Fourteenth-century manuscripts are often decorated with flowing lines that resemble light, elegant **Gothic fan-vaulting**. In the early Middle Ages, artists often simplified or exaggerated the images they created – rather like modern cartoons – to make a strong statement. Towards the end of the Middle Ages, they copied fashionable artists, who aimed to paint in a realistic style.

Works of value

The materials used to create books and manuscripts were very expensive. It could take months or years to copy and illustrate a text. Because of this, and because of their holy content, books produced in monasteries were extremely valuable. Some, such as Bibles and missals (books with the words of Christian worship), were designed for use in churches. The finest examples were covered in bindings decorated with gold and precious stones. Others, such as psalters (collections of psalms) and Books of Hours (prayers to be read privately), were produced for wealthy customers, especially noble ladies, after around 1350. They were often decorated with jewel-like pictures of flowers, insects and birds.

The wider world

Throughout the Middle Ages, European merchants travelled long distances to the Middle East and North Africa, to meet and do business with traders from many different Asian lands. They wanted to buy valuable Asian produce, especially silk cloth made in China, spices grown in India and south-east Asia, and perfumes, pearls, gold and precious stones from Arabia and Ceylon (Sri Lanka).

▼ The Italian city of Venice, around 1338. Venice was the richest, most powerful port in the Mediterranean region. Venetian merchants travelled to Russia and further east to buy silk from China, jewels from India and spices from South-East Asia.

Dangerous ways

Travel was slow, difficult and often dangerous. Roads were pot-holed and muddy; bandits (robbers) lurked alongside. Rich and **noble** men rode on horseback while noble ladies travelled in curtained litters (covered couches that were carried). Most ordinary people travelled on foot.

Ships were the best way of carrying bulky loads, but shipwrecks and pirate attacks were constant dangers. International traders travelled along two well-established routes – the Silk Route that ran overland from Constantinople to China, and the Spice Route, an ocean passage from the Red Sea to South-East Asia.

The canals are like streets in other cities – Venetians travel along them in boats

The city houses are built on islands in a shallow lagoon

There is a bridge across the canal

Merchants own grand houses with showrooms to display imported goods

There are merchant ships in the harbour

New styles from overseas

These trading ventures introduced new materials and artistic styles to Christian Europe. They included rich Middle Eastern damask cloths (woven all in one colour, but with a light-reflecting pattern), intricate Slav metalwork from Russia and eastern Europe, and Muslim **ceramics** decorated with geometric patterns. All these were copied by European artists, especially in countries with citizens belonging to several different cultural communities, such as south Italy or southern Spain.

Travellers' tales

The most famous medieval traveller was Marco Polo (1254–1324). He travelled with merchants from the Italian city of Venice all the way to China, and returned home with fascinating stories of the peoples he had met and the places he had seen. He dictated these to a **scribe**, and the resulting book soon became famous and was copied many times.

Marco Polo's book inspired other, less truthful, travellers' tales. These were often illustrated with pictures of fantastic monsters, jumbled together from descriptions of real-life exotic animals, such as elephants and giraffes. Some also included pictures of dog-headed people, and men and women with faces in their chests, or feet so big that they used them as sunshades. The most popular of these tales of imaginary travels was written by the Englishman Sir John Mandeville in the fourteenth century. Similar pictures appeared in 'Books of Wonders', which were especially popular in France.

▼ A sea-horse, from a book on the natural world written by famous medieval scholar Albertus Magnus, who lived from 1206 to 1280. Medieval travellers feared meeting monsters like this if they ventured too far from home.

▼ In this picture of a popular Bible story, painted in northern France in about 1475, three kings have followed a star to find baby Jesus, and honour him.

The king takes off his hat (with crown) in a gesture of respect

The third king has a gift of myrrh, a bitter medicine

The second king carries a gift of sweet-smelling frankincense

The first king kneels to offer a gift of gold to baby Jesus

The stable where Jesus was said to have been born

This is Joseph, husband of the Virgin Mary

Here is the Virgin Mary, Jesus' mother

Meeting other peoples

Long-distance trade brought Europeans into contact with people from different ethnic groups. There was no racial discrimination against most non-Europeans, although they were often regarded as exotic curiosities. A few late medieval artists included admiring portraits of black people in their work. However, black was also the colour traditionally used by medieval artists to show sin, and this may have influenced people's attitudes.

International scholarship

Medieval scholars in Christian Europe were trained by the Church. They spent much of their time in remote monasteries or in universities. Most countries had only two or three universities in medieval times but scholars were not isolated. They wrote letters to distant colleagues, and received replies. They felt kinship with Christian thinkers who had lived in earlier centuries, and whose works they still treasured. Even more important, they travelled long distances to meet other scholars, and to consult books in libraries.

▼ This copy of the *Canon of Medicine* by Ibn Sina (980–1037) was made in Damascus, Syria, in the 1300s. Copies of important books like this were made for use throughout the Muslim world, from southern Spain to Central Asia.

Muslim learning

This long-distance travel brought Europeans educated in the Christian tradition into contact with people of other faiths. In particular, they received new information from Muslim and Jewish scholars living in Islamic lands from southern Spain to the borders of China.

Muslim scholars were famous for their scientific investigations and discoveries, especially in astronomy, mathematics, navigation, engineering, chemistry and medicine. One Christian king, Roger II of Sicily (1093–1154), invited the Muslim geographer Al-Idrisi to live at his court and compile a world map for him. Muslim scholars also lectured at Spanish and Italian universities. One Christian professor complained that they were so good that students were ignoring other teachers.

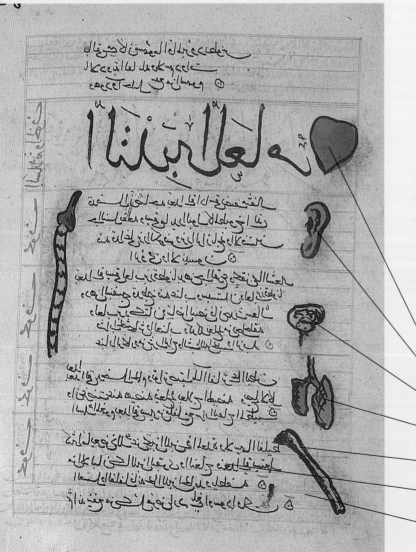

Heart

Ear

Brain

Lungs

Bone

Arabic writing, used by all Muslim scholars

Lines ruled by hand keep the writing neat on the page

New to Europe

Muslim experts introduced new technologies to Christian Europe, such as the water-wheel, used to drive irrigation (land-watering) schemes in southern Spain. From India, Muslim mathematicians brought new symbols for numbers and a way of showing zero. These revolutionized calculations, and led to many mathematical discoveries. We still use them today – and we call them 'Arabic' numbers.

European sailors learned how to use the Muslim astrolabe, an instrument that helped them work out their position at sea. European doctors translated textbooks by Muslim medical scientists to learn how to use new surgical instruments. They also improved their skills by studying case-notes published by the great Jewish physician Maimonides (1135–1204), who lived and worked in Muslim lands.

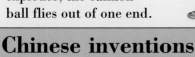

▶ This fifteenth-century gunner is setting fire to gunpowder in a hand-held cannon. As it explodes, the cannon ball flies out of one end.

Chinese inventions

China was the most technologically advanced civilization in medieval times. The Chinese invented printing, fireworks, the compass, poison gas and a machine to predict earthquakes. News of many inventions did not reach Europe. Yet knowledge of two Chinese devices, cannon and gunpowder, was brought by Muslim military engineers. They revolutionized medieval warfare. A more peaceful Chinese discovery – how to spin and weave silk thread – also came to Europe. Silk became Europe's favourite luxury fabric, and is pictured in many medieval works of art.

▼ This bell-tower, at the church of Santa Maria at Calatayud in Spain, blends European, Christian designs with Muslim styles. It was probably built by North African craftsmen.

Roman-style round arches were used in many Christian churches

The bells are for calling Christian worshippers to prayer

The tower has eight sides

The decorations are all geometric, following Muslim tradition

The tower is made of brick, a popular North African material

Multicultural art

Muslim **manuscripts** were rare in southern Europe, and so they were not often copied by Christian monks and scribes. A few examples – such as Muslim horseshoe-shaped arches decorating a page of Christian religious images – do survive. However, architects in Spain and Italy found that Muslim geometric patterns combined well with local **Romanesque** and **Gothic** designs, and used them in many of their designs.

New ideas, new explorations

After around 1400, scholars in Italy began to think about the world in a different way. At the same time, sailors and geographers based in Italy, Spain and Portugal began to make voyages of exploration to find out more about distant parts of the world. Together, these philosophical and geographical investigations led to a whole new way of looking at the world – and to the end of the Middle Ages.

▼ *The School of Athens*, by Italian Renaissance artist Raphael (1483–1520). In this painting, Raphael aimed to re-create a scene from the famous Academy (university) in Athens, Greece, founded by the philosopher Plato (c.427/8 – 348/7 BC), but he based his work on ancient Roman, rather than ancient Greek designs.

Human values

The Italian scholars' new ideas were based on writings by ancient Greek and Roman authors. Many of these pre-Christian works had been forgotten by Europeans since the collapse of the Roman Empire. Once they were read in Europe again, they had a powerful impact. They encouraged people to turn away from the religious view of life taught by the **Christian Church**, and to value human intelligence more highly. They inspired artists to appreciate the beauty of the human body, instead of seeing it as sinful, as the Church had claimed.

The use of perspective (mathematical drawing technique) creates a lifelike sense of three-dimensional space (unlike most medieval images)

This is a Roman-style stone statue

The huge arches are supported by pillars, in ancient Roman style

People are dressed in ancient Greek and Roman-style robes

People are painted to look lifelike and three-dimensional, unlike most medieval images

The professor holds a book

The Renaissance

This new movement soon had a name – the **Renaissance** (rebirth). Renaissance artists such as Leonardo da Vinci (1452–1519) and Michelangelo (1475–1564) abandoned medieval styles of painting and carving, as well as medieval subject-matter. They took special care to portray the world with scientific accuracy, and studied the human body, together with plants, rocks and animals, so that they could depict 'real' people and landscapes. They also examined the remains of ancient buildings, and dug up ancient statues and carvings, to learn from the skills of artists who had lived over a thousand years before.

Explorations

From around 1420, Portuguese sailors sailed south, in search of a sea-route to Asia. In 1488 Bartolomeu Dias rounded the Cape of Good Hope and proved that India could be reached using this route. Vasco da Gama succeeded in reaching India in 1498. This was the start of a whole new era in international trade. Six years earlier, in 1492, Christopher Columbus, an Italian adventurer funded by the Spanish king and queen, had sailed westwards across the Atlantic Ocean. He thought he had reached China but had actually arrived in a continent previously unknown to Europeans – America.

Church changes

There were also many new religious ideas in late medieval Europe. From the late fourteenth century, groups of Christian protesters called for reform in the Church. Scholars like the Dutchman Desiderius Erasmus (1469–1536) accused Church leaders of laziness, corruption and greed. They also criticized Christian believers for idolatry (worshipping artistic images, instead of God) and **superstition**. Soon after 1500, these protests led to major upheavals in European religion – and in religious art.

▼ A woodcut (print made from a block of wood carved with an image) showing King Ferdinand of Spain with Christopher Columbus's three ships. It was printed in 1493, just one year after Columbus reached America.

This is a tropical rainforest tree

Some of the native American people

These are native American houses

King Ferdinand of Spain. With his wife, Queen Isabella, he paid for Columbus's voyages

Columbus's ships have anchored in the Caribbean

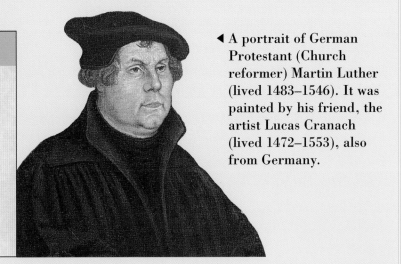

◀ A portrait of German Protestant (Church reformer) Martin Luther (lived 1483–1546). It was painted by his friend, the artist Lucas Cranach (lived 1472–1553), also from Germany.

Maps and printing

Fifteenth-century explorations changed medieval people's ideas about the world, and their own place in it. They also created a new kind of art — beautiful, scientific maps and globes.

The real world

Before around 1500, medieval maps were based on religion, rather than accurate geography. They often showed the holy city of Jerusalem at the centre of the world, and paradise (heaven) as a real island, surrounded by a dangerous ocean full of sea-monsters. Medieval geographers knew of only three continents — Europe, Africa and Asia. Most realized that the world was round, but thought it was much smaller than its actual size.

All this was changed by Portuguese voyages, which showed how long it took to sail to Asia, and by Spanish explorers who realized they had found a continent never previously discovered by Europeans. They named it America. The first map to show the continent was made in Spain around 1500, and the first globe with the same information around 1510. Both show parts of the Caribbean and the South American coast, labelled *Novus Mundus* (New World).

▶ A section of the Cantino World Map, produced in 1502.

Caribbean Islands

Tropic of Cancer

North coast of South America

The line dividing overseas lands claimed by Spain from those claimed by Portugal

Tropic of Capricorn

New technology

Another invention, printing with movable type, brought even more dramatic changes. It was invented by the German metalworker Johannes Gutenberg (c.1398 to c.1468). He **cast** individual letters from molten (melted) metal by pouring it into hollowed-out wooden blocks. He then arranged the cooled, solid metal letters in rows to make words, and placed the rows in frames to make pages.

Printing was the most exciting new technology of its day, and just as influential as the modern Internet. It allowed information about new ideas, and criticisms of old ones, to spread much more quickly and accurately than ever before. Single sheets, pamphlets and whole books could now be produced in multiple copies. This was much cheaper and quicker than copying texts slowly and painstakingly, by hand.

Images could also be combined with text, to create cheap illustrated books – and also calendars, song-sheets and playing cards. By the year 1500, about six million books had been printed – far more than all the manuscripts written during the thousand years of the Middle Ages.

Spreading the word

Kings and church leaders soon realized how dangerous printing might be in spreading challenges to their authority. Presses could be used by anyone who knew how to work them, or could pay for type, ink and paper. They tried to restrict its use by insisting that printers were licensed, but they failed. Printing had changed the world – for ever.

▶ A printing press belonging to Johannes Gutenberg, made in Germany around 1468.

The lever is pulled sideways, to lower the press on to the paper and forme

The paper is placed here

The forme (frame containing type) is put here

Ink is spread over the type

The press pushes the paper down

The forme slides into position under the paper and press

Timeline

330
Roman Empire divided into eastern and western parts; start of **Byzantine Empire** in the east

476
last Roman emperor forced to flee from Rome; western Roman Empire collapses

520–26
mosaics showing scenes from life of Jesus Christ used to decorate church in Ravenna, Italy

800
Charlemagne, king of the Franks, takes the title of Holy Roman Emperor

c.800
Celtic-style Christian books: *Book of Kells* and *Lindisfarne Gospels* produced

c.800 to c.1100
Viking raids in many parts of Europe

c.805
Charlemagne's chapel (Aachen, Germany) built, based on ancient Roman designs

828
St Mark's cathedral (Venice, Italy): building begins, in Byzantine style

c.1000
first wooden castles built

1066
Norman conquest of England

1093
Durham Cathedral (England): building begins, in **Romanesque** style

1096 to 1291
Crusaders invade Muslim lands

c.1100
first stone castles built

1163
Chartres Cathedral (France): building begins, in **Gothic** style

c.1200
first 'concentric' castles built

c.1200 to 1400
many new universities founded

1238
Alhambra Palace, Spain: building begins, in Muslim style

1248
Cologne Cathedral, Germany: building begins, in Gothic style

c.1271–95
Marco Polo's travels to and within China

1283 to 1323
one of last great fortress castles built, at Caernarvon, Wales

1337–1453
Hundred Years' War between England and France

c.1340
illustrated manuscript, the *Luttrell Psalter*, painted in England; it contains many images of peasant life

1347–51
first, and worst, outbreak of plague throughout Europe (known later as the Black Death)

c.1350
cannon used in European wars

c.1395
icon-like image (called the *Wilton Diptych*) painted; shows King Richard II of England with angels and saints

c.1400
castles now built as high-status homes, rather than fortresses

c.1400
in Italy, artists begin to develop new **Renaissance** ideas and designs

c.1410
Book of Hours, the *Très Riches Heures* of the duc de Berry, painted in France

c.1430–60
artists in northern Europe, such as Jan van Eyck and Rogier Van der Weyden, paint in very detailed, realistic style

1430
fellowship of the Golden Fleece founded in Burgundy (now Belgium/France)

1446 to 1515
one of last great Gothic churches, King's College Chapel, built in Cambridge, England

1453
Constantinople, capital of the Byzantine Empire, captured by Muslim Turks

1455
first Bible printed by Johannes Gutenberg in Mainz, Germany

1469–92
Lorenzo the Magnificent, ruler of Florence, Italy, encourages many great Renaissance-style buildings and works of art

1492
Italian sailor Christopher Columbus reaches the Americas

1497
Renaissance artist Leonardo da Vinci paints fresco, *The Last Supper*, in Italy

1498
Portuguese sailor Vasco da Gama reaches India

1498
Renaissance artist Michelangelo carves *Pietà* statue in Italy

Glossary

bishop senior priest in charge of the Church's work in a city or district

Byzantine Empire empire that ruled the Eastern Mediterranean region from 330 to 1453

cast formed by pouring melted metal into a mould

Celtic relating to a civilization that flourished throughout north and west Europe from around 800 to 50 BC.

ceramics objects made from clay

Christian Church religious organization founded by followers of Jesus Christ

chronicles written records of important events

cloisters covered walkways surrounding a central courtyard; part of a cathedral, monastery or nunnery

coat of arms design that is a special symbol of a family, city or other organization

counting house room in a merchant's house or warehouse for keeping accounts and storing money

doom medieval name for the end of the world

embroidered decorated with a pattern created by stitches in coloured or metallic thread

estate large area of land belonging to one family or organization

fan vaulting an elaborate, decorative roof structure in which the ribs supporting an arched ceiling spread outwards like fans

fellowship brotherhood; community group

fresco picture painted directly on a wall or ceiling

Gothic style of art and architecture common in Europe from around 1200 to 1450, featuring slender, pointed designs

keep strong central tower of a castle

knight title showing high social rank

manuscript text written by hand

members of parliament representatives of country districts and large towns, who discussed government policy but could be overruled by the king

missionary religious teacher who spreads their faith

moat deep ditch filled with water

mosaic picture made from tiny pieces of coloured stone, clay tile or glass

noble member of the highest class of society

pagan person who was neither a Jew, Christian or Muslim

patron wealthy person who orders and pays for a work of art or architecture

peasant country-dweller; farm worker

persecution treatment of people in a cruel or unfair way because of their religion or political beliefs, for example

priest Christian religious leader, who preaches and performs sacraments (holy ceremonies)

relics physical remains

Renaissance the revival of art and literature, influenced by ancient Greek and Roman ideas

Romanesque style of architecture common in Europe from around 900 to 1200 featuring heavy, rounded designs

saint holy person, honoured by the Christian Church

scribe person who wrote out manuscripts

superstition the belief that particular events bring good or bad luck

tapestry woven picture

toll charge for using a bridge or road

Further resources

Books

Bartlett, Robert, *Medieval Panorama* (Thames and Hudson, 2001)

Evans, Joan, *The Flowering of the Middle Ages* (Thames and Hudson, 1969)

Loyn, H. R. (Editor), *The Middle Ages: A Concise Encylopaedia* (Thames and Hudson, 1991)

Martindale, Andrew, *Gothic Art* (Thames and Hudson, 1967)

Zarnecki, George, *Romanesque Art* (Thames and Hudson, 1971)

Websites

http://www.msu.edu/~georgem1/history/medieval.htm
Part of the WWW Virtual library – a massive resource

http://www.fordham.edu/halsall/sbook.html
Medieval history sourcebook – copies and translations of many medieval texts, plus useful links

http://georgetown.edu/labyrinth/
Many medieval topics – has link to long list of 'medieval studies for kids and young adults'

http://www.ceu.hu/medstud/manual/MMM/index.html
'Medieval Manuscript Manual' – all about medieval manuscripts

http://scholar.chem.nyu.edu
A medieval technology timeline

http://www.learner.org/exhibits/middleages/
Daily life in the Middle Ages

Index

Anglo-Saxons 8, 11
architecture 4, 9, 23, 29
armour 12, 13, 16, 17

Bible 11, 19, 31, 35
books 31, 34–5, 37, 43
Byzantine Empire 4, 9, 18

castles 13, 14–15, 16
cathedrals 5, 19, 22–3
Celtic style 19
Charlemagne 9, 12
children 24, 25, 30
Chinese civilization 4, 39
chivalry 16–17
Christian ceremonies 20–1
Christian Church 7, 9, 10, 16, 18,
    22, 40
churches 9, 11, 19, 25
cloth 27, 28, 29, 36, 37
coats of arms 7, 17, 35
Columbus, Christopher 41
craftspeople 5, 29, 31
crucifixes 20, 21
Crusades 12, 18

da Vinci, Leonardo 41

education 25, 38
emperors 8, 9
entertainment 17, 32
exploration 40, 42

families 30–1
farming 26, 27

festivals 32

Gothic style 5, 23, 25, 35, 39
Gutenberg, Johannes 43

houses and homes 15, 29, 30–1

invasions 8–9

Jesus Christ 7, 18, 19, 20, 21, 27, 31
Jews 18, 19, 38

kings 7, 9, 10–11, 16, 17, 32
knights 12, 13, 15, 16–17, 26

laws 10, 11
lords 7, 26, 27

manufacturing 29
Marco Polo 37
markets 28–9
marriage 30, 31
materials 5, 11, 23, 35, 37
mathematics 39
medicine 39
merchants 29, 36–7
metalworking 9
Michelangelo 41
migrations 8
missionaries 18, 25
monasteries 11, 24–5, 38
mosaics 9, 18
mosques 9, 18
Muslims 4, 9, 12, 18, 19, 38, 39

nobles 10, 12, 15, 17, 26, 30, 32
Norman Conquest 14

patrons 7, 25, 30
peasants 12, 26–7, 31
pilgrimages 21
plague 33
printing 43

relics 21
Renaissance 4
Roman Empire 4, 8, 9, 40
Romanesque style 22, 23, 25, 35, 39

saints 7, 11, 19, 21, 24, 25, 31, 32
shops 29
stained glass 5, 17, 19, 23
symbols 7, 8, 11

tapestries 14, 17, 32
taxes 10, 26
technology 39, 43
tournaments 7, 17
towns and cities 28–9
trade 28–9, 36–7
travel 36–7, 38

Vikings 9, 10
Virgin Mary 7, 19, 21, 33

warriors 8, 9, 17
wars 12–13, 14
weapons 12, 13, 16
women 16, 26, 27, 30

Titles in the *History in Art* series include:

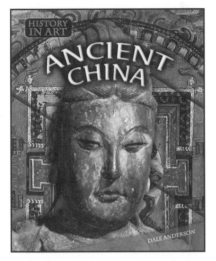

Hardback   1 844 43369 2

Hardback   1 844 43361 7

Hardback   1 844 43359 5

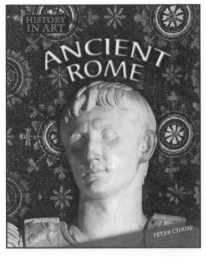

Hardback   1 844 43360 9

Hardback   1 844 43362 5

Hardback   1 844 43370 6

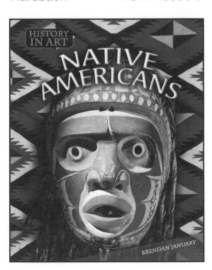

Hardback   1 844 43371 4

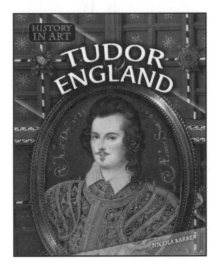

Hardback   1 844 43372 2

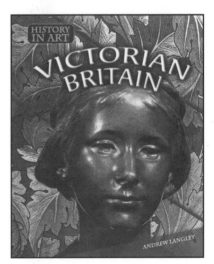

Hardback   1 844 43373 0

Find out about the other titles in this series on our website www.raintreepublishers.co.uk